Yarn CRAFTS

Plush, colorful yarn is the perfect accent for creative crafting! Wrap it around bottles or hoops, weave it through a web of spokes, bundle it into plump pom-poms — you can even tie it into your hair to turn a pony tail into a snazzy braid!

For this whimsical pony tail, tie colorful yarn to the divided sections before you begin braiding.

LEISURE ARTS, INC. • Maumelle, Arkansas

WREATH

Approximate Finished Size: 15" diameter

Shopping List

- ☐ Six coordinating yarn colors - use a mixture of thick and thin yarn in light, dark, and variegated colors (very large pom-pom: approximately 67 yards; large pom-pom: approximately 39 yards; medium pom-pom: approximately 15 yards; small pom-pom: approximately 9 yards)
- ☐ $1^5/_8$ yards of $2^1/_2$" wide wire-edge burlap ribbon
- ☐ Pom-pom makers to make pom-poms that measure approximately $3^3/_8$", $2^1/_2$", $1^5/_8$", and $1^3/_8$" in diameter
- ☐ Tan chenille stem
- ☐ 15" square of foam core board
- ☐ Craft knife
- ☐ Hot glue gun and glue sticks

To make the Wreath:

1. Cut a 13" diameter circle from the foam core board. Cut a 7" diameter circle from the center of the 13" circle.

2. Follow the manufacturer's instructions to make pom-poms in the desired sizes and colors. We made five very large pom-poms, seven large pom-poms, eleven medium pom-poms, and nine small pom-poms.

3. Cut a 3" length of ribbon; set aside. Use the remaining ribbon to make a 4-loop bow, measuring out 10" for the tails and 8" for each loop. Secure the bow with the chenille stem. Wrap the 3" ribbon length around the bow center, covering the chenille stem; glue in place.

4. Arrange the pom-poms and bow as desired on the foam core circle. Glue in place.

A.J. CRONIN
A Song of Sixpence

Dreamcatcher

Shopping List

- ☐ Steel ring (we used an 8" diameter ring and a 10" diameter ring)
- ☐ Bulky weight yarn for wrapping
- ☐ Bulky weight and/or medium weight yarns for fringe
- ☐ Crochet cotton thread for center and fringe
- ☐ Feathers and beads

To make the Dreamcatcher:

1. Wrap the ring with the bulky weight yarn, securing the beginning and ending tails under the wraps.

2. Cut a 5 yard length of crochet cotton thread and wind into a small bundle. Tie the thread to the yarn-wrapped ring *(Fig. 1)*.

Fig. 1

3. Wrap the thread around the ring and go through the loop *(Fig. 2)*; pull the "knot" tight against the ring. Continue to "knot" the thread onto the ring about every $2^1/_2$"-4" (closer together on the smaller ring, further apart on the larger ring) until you have "knotted" 8 times.

Fig. 2

4. When you reach the beginning, wrap the working thread around the thread between the "knots" on the ring and go through the loop *(Fig. 3)*; pull the "knot" against the thread. Continue around the ring, "knotting" on each thread.

Fig. 3

5. Continue "knotting" the bundled thread around the threads of the previous round until the ring is filled. Securely knot the thread and trim the excess.

6. Cut 36" lengths of yarn (and thread, if using) for fringe. Fold in half; loop and knot the yarn over the ring along the bottom *(Fig. 4)*. Add as much fringe as you like, mixing the yarn (and thread) as desired (and holding multiple strands together as desired when looping). Tie feathers and beads on the fringe and at the center as desired.

Fig. 4

7. Make a hanger by looping and knotting a 14" length of yarn (or use 2 lengths) around the ring at the top. Knot the yarn ends together.

Pom-Pom Wall Hanging

Approximate Finished Size. 17" wide x 22" high

Shopping List

- ☐ Four coordinating super bulky yarn colors - approximately 186 yards each of three colors and 268 yards of a variegated color
- ☐ $15\frac{1}{2}$" x $19\frac{1}{2}$" piece of 3.75-mesh latch hook rug canvas
- ☐ 4" x 3" piece of sturdy mat board or cardboard
- ☐ Duct tape in a coordinating color

To make the Wall Hanging:

1. Refer to **Fig. 1** to cut a rectangular hole in the mat board piece.

Fig. 1

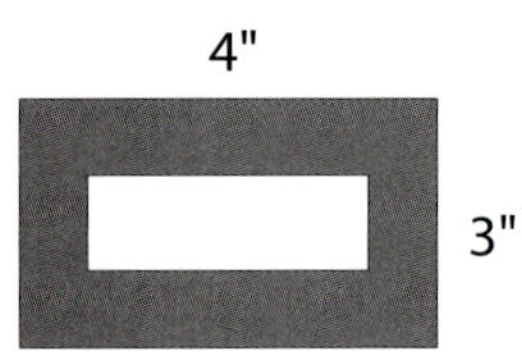

2. For each pom-pom, wrap the yarn around the mat board 60 times. Trim the yarn from the skein. Tie the yarn wraps at the center with a 12" yarn length ***(Fig. 2)***. Cut the yarn loops on each long edge of the mat board. Fluff out the pom-pom and trim as desired; do **not** trim the center tying yarn. Make 25 variegated yarn pom-poms and 17 pom-poms from each solid color yarn.

Fig. 2

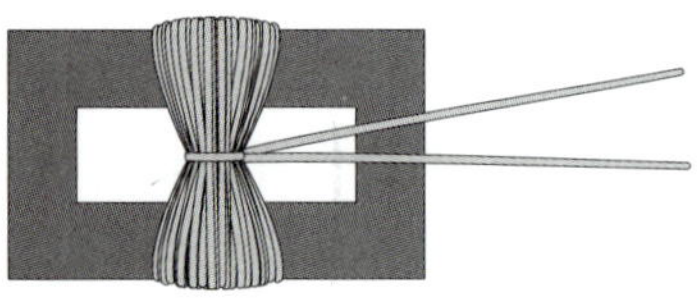

3. Folding the duct tape in half, cover the edges of the rug canvas with duct tape ***(Fig. 3)***.

Fig. 3

4. Beginning at one corner and making 2 rows of pom-poms slightly off set from one another, securely tie all the pom-poms of one color to the rug canvas along one long side ***(Figs. 4-5)***.

Fig. 4

Fig. 5

5. Continue tying the pom-poms to the canvas, creating 3 rows of the variegated pom-poms and 2 rows of the remaining solid color pom-poms.

MOORE
THE GREEN BERETS
CROWN

Arrow WALL HANGING

Shopping List

- ☐ Unfinished wood arrow (ours is 19" long)
- ☐ Teal super bulky weight yarn - approximately 9 yards
- ☐ Cream super bulky weight yarn - approximately 13 yards
- ☐ Eight 1/2" diameter natural-colored wood beads
- ☐ Glossy woodtone spray

To make the Arrow:

1. Follow the manufacturer's instructions to apply two coats of glossy woodtone spray to the arrow, being sure to cover the sides. Allow to dry.

2. Cut 13 20" lengths of the teal yarn and 20 20" lengths of cream yarn. Starting at one end with a teal yarn length, fold the yarn in half, loop, and knot the yarn around the arrow shaft ***(Fig. 1)*** in the following order: 4 teal, 10 cream, 5 teal, 10 cream, 4 teal.

Fig. 1

3. Slide each bead on a yarn end as desired. Trim the bottom yarn ends to a chevron.

DOWEL WALL HANGING

You can also loop and knot 20" long cream and variegated yarn lengths onto a 12" long 3/4" diameter dowel. Hot glue wood end caps on the dowel ends. Pull 4 yarn lengths from each side to the center and secure with a mother of pearl buckle or open rectangle bead and a twig.

Yarn-Wrapped Bottles

Shopping List

- ☐ Variegated bulky weight yarn - approximately 20 yards for each bottle
- ☐ Three small glass milk bottles (ours are $6^1/_2$" high each)
- ☐ Double-sided tape
- ☐ Hot glue gun and glue sticks

To cover the Bottles:

1. Place a tape strip vertically on each bottle from the neck to the bottom. This will hold the yarn in place while you wrap.

2. For each bottle, wrap the yarn around the bottle, pressing the yarn lightly into the tape and gluing the yarn to the bottle as necessary. Be careful not to overlap the wraps.

Feather on canvas

Shopping List

- ☐ 10" x 10" x 1 3/8" stretched artist canvas
- ☐ Variegated medium weight yarn - approximately 12 yards
- ☐ 18" length of floral wire
- ☐ Acrylic paint (cream and dark tan)
- ☐ Paintbrush
- ☐ Clear acrylic spray sealer
- ☐ Liquid starch
- ☐ Wire cutters
- ☐ Hot glue gun and glue sticks

To make the Canvas:

1. Paint the canvas cream, being sure to paint the sides. Add a light coat of dark tan paint around the outer edges, brushing in a haphazard manner. Allow to dry thoroughly. Spray with acrylic sealer and allow to dry.

2. Cut the floral wire length in half. Cut 50 7" lengths of yarn. Starting about 3" from one wire end, tie the yarn lengths around the wire length. Run a very thin line of glue over the knots on the wrong side of the feather. Wrap the exposed wire end with yarn, gluing as necessary.

3. Pour the liquid starch in a shallow dish. Dip the feather into the starch and let the yarn become saturated. Squeeze out the excess starch. Place the feather on the painted canvas at a slight angle and toward the top left of the canvas. Gently pull the wrapped wire end toward the bottom right of the canvas. Use your finger to smooth and coax the yarn "feathers" into place. Allow the starch to dry. Glue any sections of the feather that are not adhered to the canvas.

WOVEN BASKET

Shopping List

- ☐ Variegated bulky weight yarn - approximately 17 yards
- ☐ Light tan bulky weight yarn - approximately 5 yards
- ☐ 4 1/2" diameter circle of sturdy corrugated cardboard
- ☐ Large eye yarn needle
- ☐ 37 2 5/8" long toothpicks
- ☐ Hot glue gun and glue sticks

To make the Basket:

1. Referring to **Fig. 1**, use a pencil to mark 37 dots around the cardboard circle about 1/8" from the outer edge.

Fig. 1

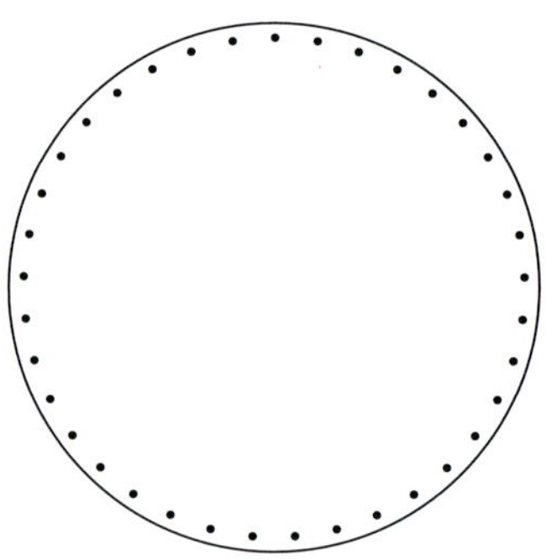

2. Using the needle to make a hole, glue a toothpick into the cardboard at each dot *(Fig. 2)*.

Fig. 2

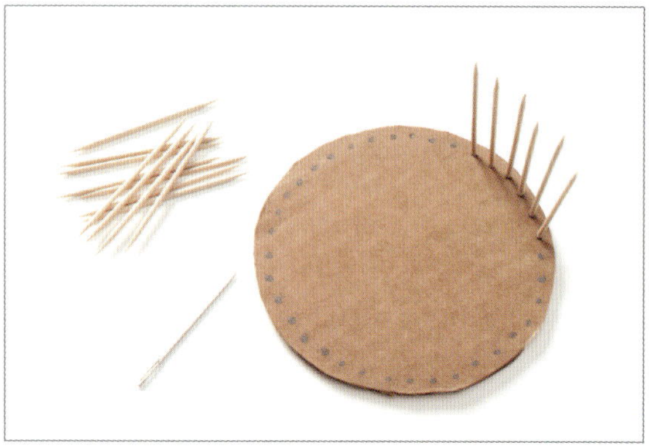

3. Cut a 3 yard length of variegated yarn and wind into a small bundle. Hot glue the yarn end to the cardboard near a toothpick. Begin weaving the yarn over and under, going around the circle *(Fig. 3)*.

Fig. 3

4. Continue weaving, tying on new lengths of yarn as necessary, until the basket is about 2 1/4" tall. Cut the yarn end and hide the end by weaving it into the woven area.

5. Refer to **Finger Crochet**, page 24, to make a variegated yarn chain long enough to go around the basket base and one to go along the top edge. Glue these lengths to the basket. Make a 20" long light tan yarn chain. Tie it around the basket near the top, gluing in place as necessary.

HOOP WALL HANGING

Shopping List

- ☐ 27" diameter plastic hoop toy
- ☐ Six-eight coordinating colors of super bulky weight yarn - approximately 17-22 yards of each yarn
- ☐ Super bulky weight yarn for foundation spokes and to wrap the hoop - approximately 42 yards

To make the Wall Hanging:

1. Tie the wrapping yarn to the hoop. Wrap the yarn around the hoop, completely covering the hoop. Knot the yarn ends together; tuck the ends under the wraps and trim the excess.

2. For the foundation spokes, cut one 40" length and sixteen 36" lengths of yarn. Knot two 36" yarn lengths together about 3" from one end. Place over the hoop and knot together at the opposite side of the hoop *(Fig. 1)*.

Fig. 1

3. Continue adding foundation spokes, working in a clockwise fashion until you have used all the 36" yarn lengths. Catching all the spokes, wrap the 40" yarn length over all the spokes at the center where they cross *(Fig. 2)*. Bring the yarn ends over the hoop edge and tie the ends together. Adjust the spokes so they are evenly spaced around the hoop.

Fig. 2

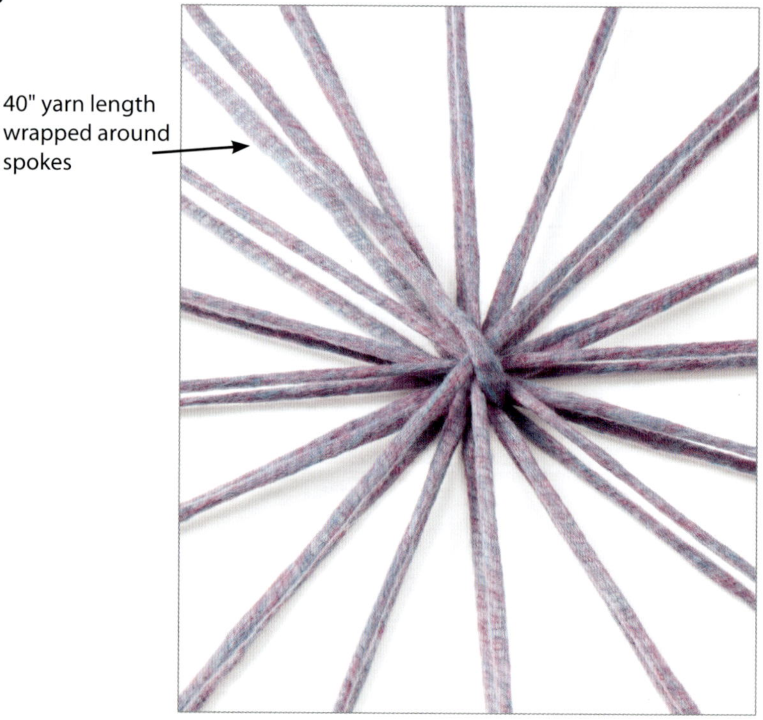

4. Cut a 10 yard length of the yarn for the center and wind it into a small bundle. Tie the yarn end to the center of the foundation spokes. Weave over and under the spokes until the center woven area is the desired size; cut the yarn, leaving about 4" to tie on the next yarn.

5. Cut a 10 yard length of the next desired color yarn. Wind it into a small bundle. Tie the yarn end to the end of the previous yarn color. Weave over and under the spokes until the woven area is the desired size; cut the yarn, leaving about 4" to tie on the next color.

6. Repeat Step 5, changing colors as desired until the hoop is about $^{2}/_{3}$ full. Cut the yarn and tie it to the nearest foundation spoke.

7. Pull all yarn ends to the wrong side of the wall hanging. Trim the foundation spoke yarn ends.

"&" Wall Art

Shopping List

- ☐ 9" x 12" unfinished wood plaque
- ☐ Thin yarn or crochet cotton thread - approximately 18-20 yards
- ☐ 17-gauge 1" long stainless wire brads - approximately 130
- ☐ White chalk-finish spray paint
- ☐ Clear acrylic spray sealer
- ☐ Painter's tape
- ☐ Hammer

To make the Wall Art:

1. Spray the wood plaque with paint. Allow to dry. Spray with sealer. Allow to dry.

2. Use a computer to print an "&" in the desired font that will fit on the plaque. Tape the paper pattern to the plaque.

3. Placing the nails about $^3/_8$" apart and leaving about $^1/_2$" of each nail above the wood, drive the nails into the plaque with the hammer along the design lines *(Fig. 1)*. After all the nails are in place, carefully remove the paper pattern

Fig. 1

4. Tie the yarn/thread end to a nail. Going back and forth as desired, wrap the yarn around the nails to "fill in" the "&" *(Fig. 2)*. Add more yarn as necessary, tying as small a knot as possible. Continue wrapping until the desired look is achieved. Tie the yarn to the nearest nail and trim.

Fig. 2

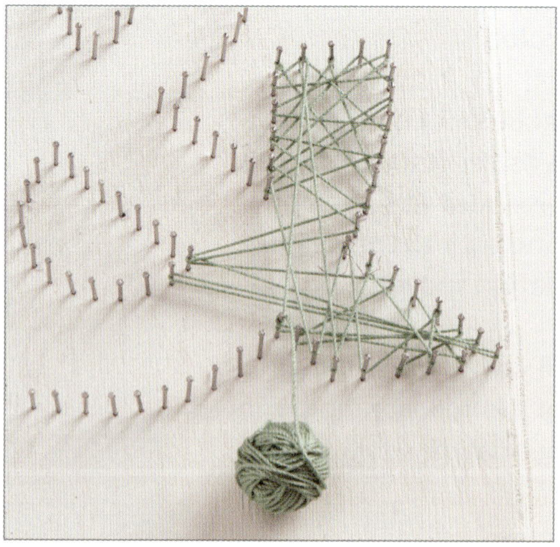

WOVEN PLACE MAT

Approximate Finished Size. 16" wide x 13" high, excluding fringe

Shopping List

- ☐ 4 coordinating bulky weight yarns - approximately 45 yards of each color (we used green, dark purple, lime, and purple/green variegated yarns)
- ☐ 20" x 15" piece of sturdy corrugated cardboard

To make the Place Mat:

1. Referring to **Fig. 1**, cut 30 slits on each end of the cardboard piece.

Fig. 1

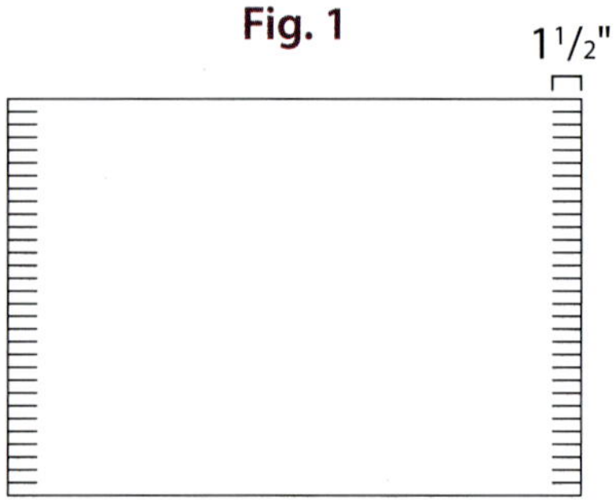

2. Cut 30 27" lengths of both the green and purple yarns. Beginning with purple and alternating colors, slip 2 lengths of yarn into each slit on either end of the cardboard ***(Fig. 2)***.

Fig. 2

3. Cut a 5 yard length of green yarn and roll into a small bundle. Leaving a 6" yarn end, weave the yarn over and under the yarn lengths on the cardboard until the green woven area is about 1" wide ***(Fig. 3)***. To tighten the weave, use your fingers to push the woven rows together. Cut the yarn leaving a 6" yarn end. The ends will be woven in later.

Fig. 3

4. Cut a 5 yard length of variegated yarn and roll into a small bundle. Weave the yarn over and under the yarn lengths on the cardboard until the variegated woven area is about 1 3/4" wide.

5. Continue weaving with the yarn colors as desired, varying the woven area widths from 3/4" to 3 1/4". Weave yarn until the entire piece of cardboard is covered.

6. Carefully remove the place mat from the cardboard. For the fringe, knot the green and purple yarn lengths together along the ends ***(Fig. 4)***. Trim the fringe to 2". Weave the remaining yarn ends into the place mat and trim.

Fig. 4

Pom-Pom Flowers

Shopping List

- ☐ Four coordinating medium weight yarn colors - approximately 15 yards for each pom-pom, plus a small amount of one color to wrap bottle neck
- ☐ Coordinating bulky weight yarn for stems and to wrap bottle
- ☐ $1^5/_8$" pom-pom maker
- ☐ 18" floral wire length for each flower
- ☐ Small glass bottle (ours is $4^1/_2$" high)
- ☐ Double-sided tape
- ☐ Wire cutters
- ☐ Hot glue gun and glue sticks

To make the Arrangement:

1. For each flower, follow the manufacturer's instructions to make a pom-pom in the desired color yarn. We made eight pom-poms.

2. For each flower stem, trim a floral wire piece to the desired length. We trimmed ours to 13", 11", 10", 9", and 7" lengths. Glue the stem yarn to one end of the wire stem. Wrap the yarn around the stem, gluing as necessary. Glue a pom-pom to each stem.

3. To decorate the bottle, wrap the bottle neck with medium weight yarn, gluing the ends in place. To wrap the main part of the bottle, place a tape strip vertically on the bottle. This will hold the yarn in place while you wrap. Wrap the bulky weight yarn around the bottle, pressing the yarn lightly into the tape and gluing the yarn to the bottle as necessary. Insert the flower stems into the bottle.

Finger Crochet

1. To start a finger crochet chain, make a slip knot about 4" from the yarn end by grabbing the yarn at the star and pulling it through the top loop *(Fig. 1)*; tighten the new loop you just made.

Fig. 1

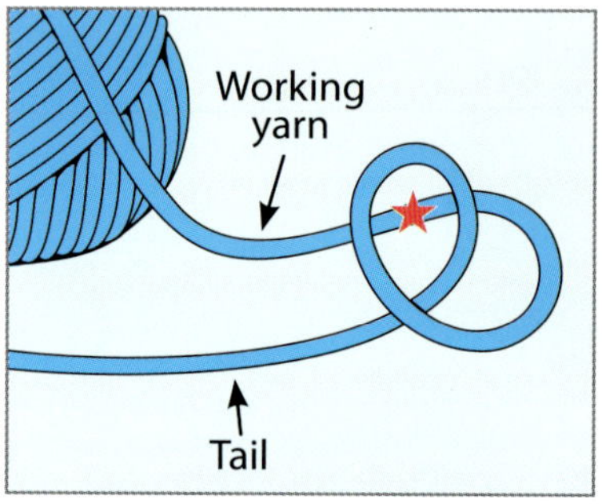

2. Grab the working yarn and pull it through the loop as indicated by the arrows ***(Fig. 2)***, creating a chain stitch *(Fig. 3)*. Tighten the new loop.

Fig. 2

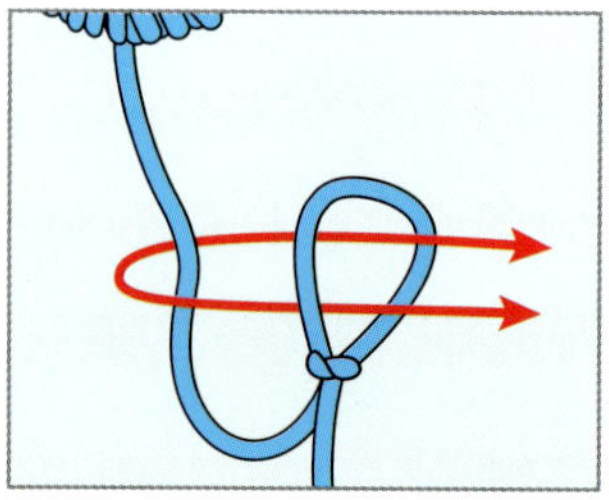

Fig. 3

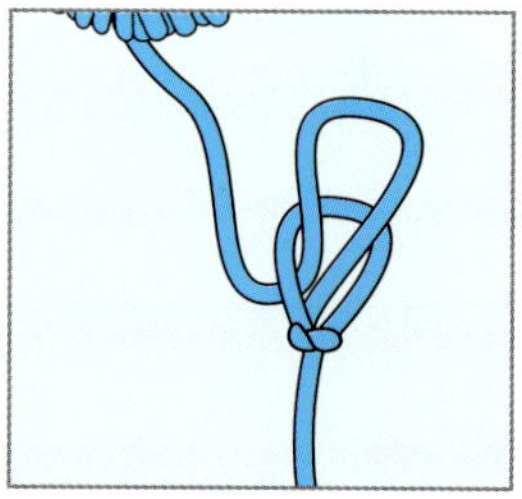

3. Continue making new chain stitches until the chain is the desired length. Trim the yarn about 4" from the last chain stitch and pull the end through that stitch *(Fig. 4)* and tighten.

Fig. 4

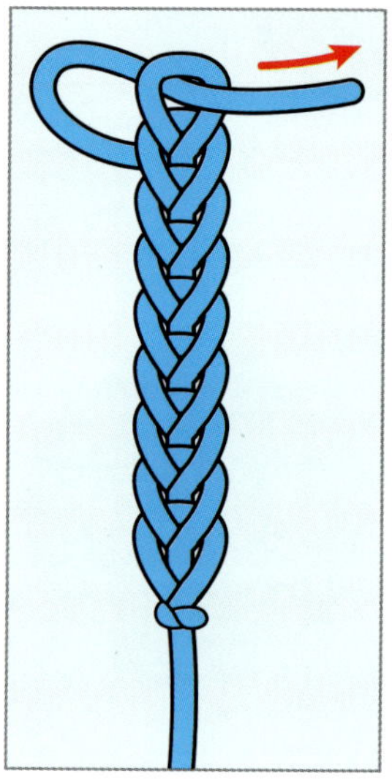

Production Team: Designer – Kelly Reider; Technical Writer – Mary Sullivan Hutcheson; Technical Associate – Jean Lewis; Editorial Writer – Susan Frantz Wiles; Senior Graphic Artist – Lora Puls; Graphic Artist – Cailen Cochran; Photostylists – Angela Alexander and Sondra Daniel ; Photographers – Jason Masters and Ken West.